WELLINGT

History, Heritage & Culture

Gavin McLean

University of Otago Press

Local Guide: Wellington

Look for these Local Guides published by University of Otago Press:
Arrowtown, Dunedin, The Catlins, Oamaru, Queenstown, Stewart Island, Wanaka.

Dedicated to Caitlin McCracken Kelly as a record of her city in the year of her birth, and of what her parents Michael and Helen are fighting to save.

Published by University of Otago Press
Level 1/398 Cumberland Street, Dunedin, New Zealand
Fax: 64 3 479 8385. Email: university.press@stonebow.otago.ac.nz

Copyright © Gavin McLean 2004
First published 2004, ISBN 1 877276 95 2

Printed by Spectrum Print Ltd, Christchurch

Unless otherwise indicated, all photographs are by the author.

Cover photographs
Front: Looking across the Clyde Quay boat harbour to the Freyberg Pool and St Gerard's monastery.
Back, top: Arts Festival banners, Frank Kitts Park.
Back, bottom: Jackson Street's restored police station and gaol is a focal point of the heritage precinct in Lower Hutt.
Page 1: Enjoying sun and sea at the Taranaki Street wharf.

The City to Sea bridge connects Civic Square to the waterfront

Contents

Nikau palms, Civic Square.

1   A Short History *page 7*

2   Harbour City, City Highlights *page 13*
        Cable Car, Botanic Garden and Thorndon Walk 13;
        Parliamentary Precinct Walk 19; A Walk along 'the
        Beach': Lambton Quay 23; Cuba Street and Courtenay
        Place Stroll 26

3   Harbour City, Harbour Highlights *page 33*
        Waterfront Walk 33; Southern Coast Drive and Red
        Rocks Walk 42; Boat Trip to Matiu/Somes Island 47;
        Eastern Bays Excursion 48

4   Best of the Rest *page 53*
        Museums, Galleries and Historic Places 53; Nature and
        Nurture 59

      Maps
        Wellington City 4–5; Wellington Harbour 30–31;
        Botanic Garden 63; Wellington Region 64

The Beehive, seat of power.

Information/Getting Around

Compact, hemmed in between harbour and hills, Wellington has an excellent public transport system. It can get you at or near virtually everything featured in this book. For further information, go to the Regional Council's Ridewell website www.wrc.govt.nz/rt/ridewell.html, phone Ridewell on 801-7000, or pick up timetables from: the Visitor Centre in Civic Square (Ph. 802-4860), the Railway Station, Public Library foyer, Cable Car terminus, or selected newsagents. The 'City Circular' bus links most central city attractions.

Central Wellington is great for walking or mountain biking. Visit or contact the Visitor Centre: Ph. 802-4860 or www.wellingtonnz.com/Bookings VisitorCentre/ about tour packages and for free leaflets on heritage and arts trails.

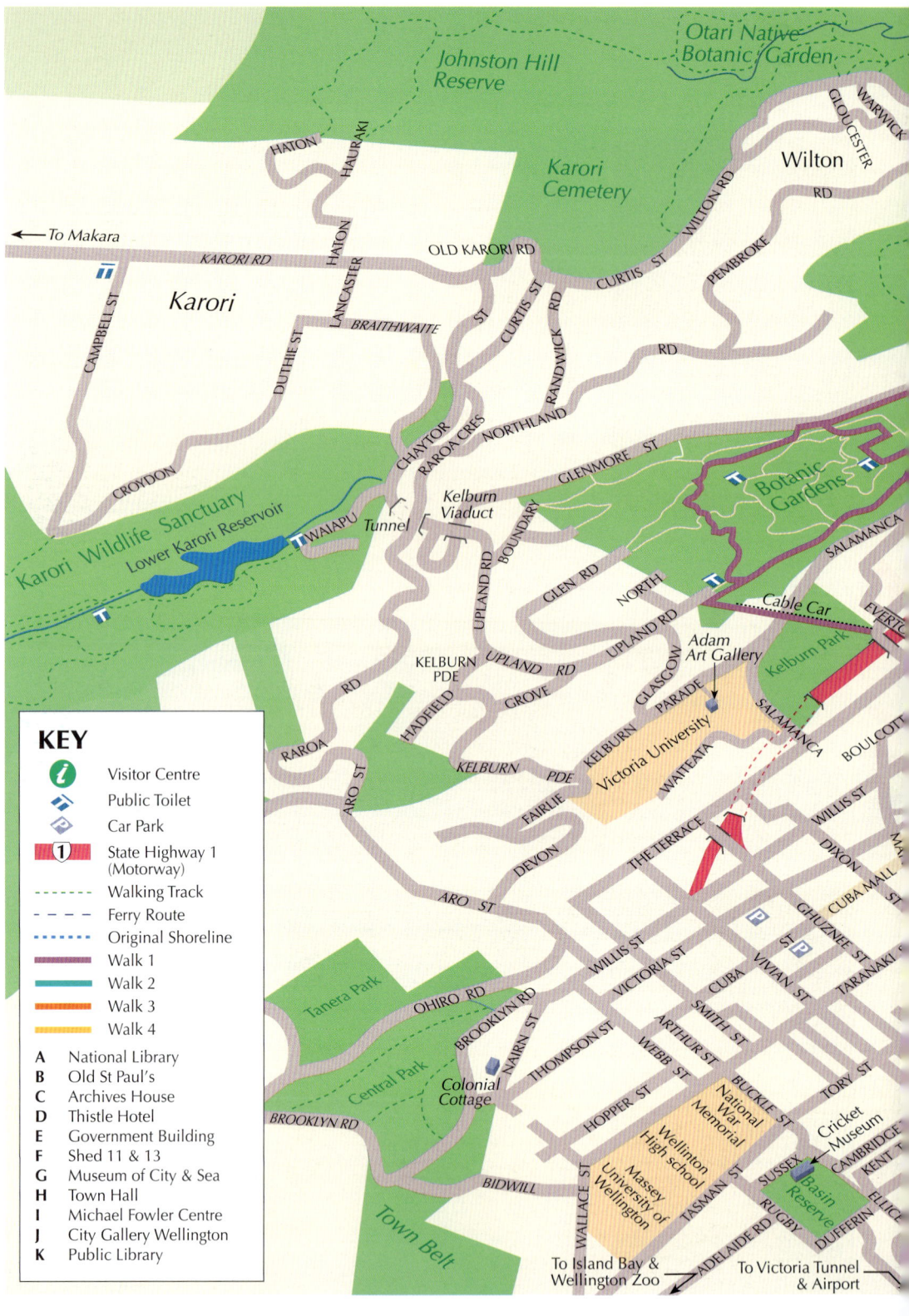

WELLINGTON 5

1: A Short History

'I wish I was in Wellington, the wind it cuts right through/I wish I was in Wellington, there's so much more to do'. The Muttonbirds capture the edgy feel of a city that parties on shaky ground in Nature's biggest wind tunnel. In 1840 Lieutenant Best, an unhappy camper with the first very unsettled settlers, despaired as spring gales shrieked interminably. 'When will these winds cease?' One night 'my [tent] poles were screwed round and round and I bolted out just in time to save its coming down about my ears'. Then there were the earthquakes. He woke up dreaming of bells, only to discover that the sound was coming from bottles rattling under his bed!

But as we shall see, the Harbour City's splendours more than compensate for the odd gale or tremor. *Suprema a situ*, supreme by position, the city motto proclaims. Travel writer Jan Morris praised a city that 'stands like a noble bowl among its surrounding mountains. It looks symmetrical, purposeful, altogether functional… it might have been scooped out by a million bull-dozers'.

Polynesians had been getting used to the place for 500 years before Ensign Best got his poles in a twist. The earliest known name for Wellington, is 'Te Upoko o te Ika a Maui' or 'the head of Maui's fish', as legend describes the North Island, pulled up by Maui. Kupe and Ngahue, Polynesian navigators, were early visitors. Later still, Tara and Tautoke, the sons of Whatonga from the Mahia peninsula, encouraged their father to establish a settlement around 'Te Whanganui a Tara', the Great Harbour of Tara. And great it was, rich in food resources, perched astride the trade

Left: Kupe, the legendary Polynesian discoverer, is commemorated on the waterfront by W.T. Trethewey's 1940 Centennial Exhibition statue, now bronzed.

It looks impressive, but the painting below was New Zealand Company propaganda. The artist has exaggerated the width of the Hutt Valley, turned its hills into molehills and broadened the Hutt River to suggest that it was navigable. Burnham Water, drained over a hundred years ago, is on the Miramar Peninsula (foreground).
Alexander Turnbull Library C-029-006-b

routes. And the war paths. Ngati Ira from the East Coast had lost ground in the early 1800s and Ngati Mutenga fled to the Chathams in 1835, leaving Te Ati Awa from Taranaki top dogs. But the malevolent spectre of Te Rauparaha and his Ngati Toa warriors just north at Kapiti gave them reason to welcome outsiders.

Those newcomers in 1840 were British colonists, the New Zealand Company's guinea pigs for Edward Gibbon Wakefield's systematic colonisation theory. The Wellington experiment showed that it was not possible to send out Wakefield's desired orderly slice of British society (the poor were too poor to go and the rich were happy to stay put). Nor could the company keep land prices sufficiently 'sufficient' (i.e. high) to cover its overheads. It also botched the purchase of land from the Maori and its subsequent surveying. And Maori, used to token Europeans living on Maori terms, were horrified when shiploads of settlers began to swamp them. In the cultural equivalent of plate tectonics, this British plate crunched over the Maori one, 'shattering dreams, power bases, reputations, fortunes – and a few heads'.

Wakefield also failed to make Wellington the capital, but he did found New Zealand's largest European settlement of the day. The great earthquakes of 1848 and 1855 knocked confidence and discouraged people from building in brick, giving the town a curiously impermanent air. Wellington's big opportunity came in 1865, when South Island politicians helped along the relocation of the capital to this more central location. The city still lives and breathes politics.

From the late 1870s, when the first trains began running over the Rimutakas to Featherston, Wellington industry took off, as its great harbour now had cheap, efficient links to the rural hinterland. The city trailed the other main centres until the

Wellington 1842. The first part of William Mein Smith's panorama shows (above) houses along the foreshore of Lambton Quay and Thorndon. Even then this was the 'official' end of town. Features include The Terrace, Kumutoto Point and pa, Colonel Wakefield's house, Barrett's hotel, the immigration barracks and the flagstaff. Te Aro Flat was the commercial end of town and the second part of the panorama (opposite, top) looks out over from Windy Point (modern Stewart Dawson's Corner) across Te Aro to Mount Albert and Mount Cook. The shoreline approximately follows modern Willis Street. Alexander Turnbull Library PUBL-0011-16-1 and PUBL-0011-16-3

Queens Wharf was the hub of nineteenth-century Wellington. When William Gibb painted the city's first large public wharf in 1899, a single clipper was drying its sails in the smoky air created by the steamers. Most of the elaborate brick 'sheds' survive, although reclamation in the early 1970s pushed them back from the water's edge.
William Gibb, Alexander Turnbull Library, C-060-008

interventionist Liberal government (1890–1912) took office, creating many state jobs in the 'Empire City', as it was then called. Between 1891 and 1901 Wellington grew by 44 per cent. New drains banished its reputation as New Zealand's unhealthiest city. Above ground, tall masonry buildings replaced wooden ones. The city grew out as well as up, opening up new suburbs thanks to the cable car (1902) and the electric trams (from 1903).

Wellington was also becoming a centre of business, thanks to its port and its hold on government. In 1900 it handled twice the tonnage of shipping that Auckland did. The commercial district bloomed between the wars, bolstered by producer boards, oil companies, motor vehicle distributors and a plethora of smaller factories. At the same time, Wellington became the financial capital of New Zealand, as you will see in the buildings near the Old Bank Arcade.

Labour took office in 1935. Like the Liberals 40 years earlier, its policies were good for Wellington, pumping jobs and money into the city. Over the summer of 1939–40, 2.6 million people visited the futuristic Centennial Exhibition at Rongotai that celebrated the new welfare state. Labour's state housing, the familiar tiled cottages, replaced some of the city's worst slums, but most post-war housing occurred out in the Hutt Valley. Porirua became a centre of manufacturing and distribution, and from the late 1960s the Kapiti Coast mushroomed as a retirement or commuting area. This suburban sprawl brought transport problems. The region kept its suburban trains, but lost its trams in 1964. Elsewhere, motorways and flyovers were squeezed in where space permitted.

After 1945 the city's population took on new hues. Maori, almost absent from the city since the 1860s, returned to take up jobs in its new factories, as did Pacific Islanders. Smaller numbers of continental Europeans also sailed in. But the factory jobs did not last long, largely axed by the free market policies of the late 1980s. Many big plants around Petone, Lower Hutt and Porirua closed their doors. By then, Wellington had finished transforming the Victorian/Edwardian character of Lambton Quay with another concrete canyon, whose new tower blocks soon found themselves hustling for tenants, as 'downsizing' caught up with white-collar workers after the 1987 sharemarket crash. At least that crash killed the crassest of the waterfront redevelopment plans. For more than a decade, citizens fought over what to do with the old port area.

SOME LOCAL NAMES

European

Wellington: named after the Duke of Wellington, British general and prime minister.

New Zealand Company officials: Lambton Harbour (the family name of the Earl of Durham); Manners Street – Frederick James Tollemache's father's name was Sir William Manners; Molesworth Street – Sir William Molesworth; Courtenay Place – Viscount Courtenay; Wakefield Street – Edward Gibbon Wakefield.

Immigrant ships: Aurora Terrace, Cuba Street, Tory Street, Oriental Bay, Glenbervie Terrace etc.

Politicians: Stout Street – Sir Robert Stout, Chief Justice; Ballance Street – John Ballance, Premier 1891–3.

Governors: Grey Street – Sir George Grey was Governor and Premier several times; Jervois Quay – Sir William Jervois was Governor 1885–90.

Maori

Te Upoko o te Ika a Maui, meaning 'the head of maui's fish', is a name for the wider Wellington area.

Whanganui-a-Tara is 'the great harbour of Tara'.

Taranaki Street was named because the inhabitants of Te Aro Pa came from that region.

In the meantime Wellington, perhaps never as grey an old civil service city as some now like to think, successfully rebranded itself as the cultural capital. The New Zealand International Arts Festival took off like a rocket. The city developed the Wellington Museum City & Sea and other specialist museums, and in 1998 the new Museum of New Zealand, Te Papa Tongarewa, opened, drawing in record numbers of visitors. Almost overnight Wellington became a major tourism destination. And local boy Peter Jackson lured in American money to make Miramar the heart of 'Wellywood', producing the *Lord of the Rings* trilogy.

In the 1990s a vibrant café culture sprang up around 'ABC' – Allen and Blair Streets and Courtenay Place – and the inner city apartment lifestyle appealed to many. Sports fans got the 'Cake Tin', the shiny new metal stadium. In 2003 the council barged 20,000 tonnes of sand from Golden Bay to widen Oriental Bay's slip of a beach. Public enterprise conserved some key icons – Parliament Buildings, Government Buildings, the Old Bank Arcade and the waterfront brick 'sheds' – though many more were demolished or desecrated by unsightly additions and alterations. Mediocrity lifts its leg over masterpieces throughout this city.

The 2001 census showed that about 340,000 people made their home in Greater Wellington, 164,000 of them in Wellington City. More European (81.7 per cent) and Asian (10.8 per cent) than average, they are wealthier and better educated. They are also more likely to be online, in one of the most 'wired' cities on Earth.

Central Wellington from the air, ca 1940. The liner Awatea *is berthed at the outer tee of Queens Wharf. The Midland Hotel (left) is now a park and Kirkcaldies' is now a façade, but many of the taller buildings south of them still survive in the twenty-first century. Notice the small size of most of the buildings on the western side of Lambton Quay.* Alexander Turnbull Library, PAColl-5469-060

2 Harbour City, City Highlights

Much of the Wellington city area can be termed a walker's city. In this chapter we outline three walking routes that will introduce you to both quaint and curious. The first two will take a morning or an afternoon, especially if you include some of the visits featured in Chapter 4, while the third will take an hour or so. Finally, a stroll around Cuba Street/Courtenay Place is suggested.

Cable Car, Botanic Garden, Historic Thorndon Walk

Cable Car Lane is on the western side of Lambton Quay, tucked away behind the snazzy cable car sign. Technically a funicular, the cable car has been here for more than a century, although the current terminus, charming as a bomb shelter, had its big makeover 30 years ago. Buy your ticket and climb aboard, thanking property speculators for one of the city's most enduring and endearing forms of transport.

Flat land has always been in short supply in Wellington. The steep hillsides above The Terrace remained empty until the Upland Estate Company's associate, the Kelburn and Karori Tramway Company Ltd, commissioned James Fulton to design a transport system to lure house buyers. Fulton, who came from Dunedin (which had a cable car), designed a cable track that was 785 metres long, climbed over 119 metres in height at an average grade of 1 in 5.1 and passed through three tunnels and over three viaducts. A steam engine powered the cable winding gear. This drove an endless wire rope (or haulage cable) which operated alternatively up one line of track and down the other. The ascending and descending cable cars counterbalanced each other.

For two and a half years work gangs, including prisoners, sweated away with shovels and wheelbarrows building the tunnels, viaducts, and laying track. On opening day, 22 February 1902, 4000 Wellingtonians gave the new service a test drive. Patronage rose steadily, from 425,000 in 1902 to over a million in 1912 and two million by the mid 1920s. Electricity replaced steam power in 1933 and the council took over in 1947.

The present cars date from 1979. The authorities banned the old trailer units in 1974 and four years later, to the dismay of many, the old cars were withdrawn. The swish Swiss cars now carry about a million passengers a year – students, residents and tourists – up and down a single track with a passing loop. After Lambton station, there are four stops, Clifton Terrace, Salamanca Road, University and Upland Road. Cars leave every ten minutes and run until 10 pm every night.

The top is dominated by a large modern (1984) tearooms and restaurant, looking a bit like a trellis octopus, successor to the historic

Million-dollar views for the price of loose change. The views from the cable car terminus are spectacular.

Kelburn Kiosk, which burned down in 1982. The viewing platforms beside the track or around the edge of the tearooms are the places to take some classic shots of Wellington.

The Wellington Cable Car Museum, opened in 2000, inhabits the old winding house, where you will find an old car, a trailer, models, and displays from the days of strap hanging. Admission is free. Open Mon–Fri 9.30 am–5 pm (5.30 pm summer), weekends and public holidays 10 am–4.30 pm. Ph. 475-3578; www.cablecarmuseum.co.nz.

It is now time to enter the Botanic Garden. As it covers 25 hectares, make sure you pick up a free pamphlet and map at either the cable car terminus or at the Cable Car Museum. The Garden began as a scientific experiment by the New Zealand Institute in 1868 and has been managed by the council since 1891. It is open from sunrise to sunset and admission is free.

As the map on page 63 shows, there are several main routes through the garden. Grass Way, a popular western one, will take you around to the Treetops Lookout and Information Centre, down through the Dell, up by the Herb Garden and down to the Begonia House. The East Path and the Norwood Path offer a chance to inspect some historic buildings while looking out over the city. Near the Cable Car Museum are several observatories and instrument stations. The striking brick building was built as the Hector Observatory in 1907. Renamed the Dominion Observatory in 1925, it kept the time for the government and from 1916 was also the first site of local seismic

At the Cable Car Museum: exploring technology of a hundred years ago.

This little observatory was originally named after the scientist Sir James Hector, who was associated with the Colonial Museum (now Te Papa Museum of New Zealand), these gardens and other city institutions.

Below: Since 2003 the observatory has been kept company by a Krupp canon, taken as a trophy at the end of the First World War.

WELLINGTON

Part of the succulent garden near the Treehouse Visitor Centre in the Botanic Garden.

research. It has been restored recently. Newer is the Carter Observatory, opened in 1941 and New Zealand's national observatory. Admission charges apply to the Carter and its planetarium: Ph. 472-8167; www.carterobs.ac.nz. Working stations include the small Thomas King Observatory and, a bit further away, the striking concrete bulk of the Met Office, which keeps a weather eye out on the country.

Whichever path you take, aim to end up in the lower garden. Here you will find several attractions including the Begonia House and Café and the Lady Norwood Rose Garden, established in 1953.

The western gate takes you out into Thorndon, one of the city's oldest suburbs, now as protected as anything can be in Wellington by the Thorndon Special Zone, after the motorway debacle of the 1960s. Two side streets on your right reward a quick detour. In Ascot Terrace, a narrow lane between the pub and a shop, beautifully cared-for cottages cram in cheek by jowl. No. 30, Granny Cooper's Cottage, dates from 1862 and is named after the woman who ran a school from this tiny cottage for 20 years from 1867.

Back on Tinakori Road, Nos 304–14 are a small clutch of tall, narrow San Francisco-style 'painted ladies'. No. 251 Tinakori Road is a small worker's cottage from the 1850s. In our second detour, follow Glenbervie Terrace (named after another early New Zealand Company ship) up and around to No. 31 Glenbervie Terrace, 'The Moorings', which dates from 1905 and was designed by J.S. Swan to incorporate nautical touches. Star of the street, though, is 'The

There are over 3600 roses in the Lady Norwood Rose Garden and the Begonia House shelters 5000 plants under its 120 square metres of Belgian glass. The buildings in the background include the historic gardener's house and on the skyline the Met Office.

With its tiny, cheek-by-jowl workers' cottages and its narrow, winding lane, Ascot Terrace is one of the highlights of Thorndon. Note the Seddon Memorial on the skyline.

Tinakori Road is an agreeable mix of restaurants, shops and residences. Most date from Victorian and Edwardian times, and are well maintained by proud owners.

Wedge', named for obvious reasons, and built by James Bennie in 1906. Follow the track around past 'The Wedge' and back on to Tinakori Road, where we will cross to the left and follow the path down to Premier House, home to many of the country's leaders since the capital moved down from Auckland. After Labour's first Prime Minister, Michael Joseph Savage, refused to live in anything so grand in 1935, it became a dental clinic but it was restored again as a prime ministerial residence in time for the 1990 sesquicentennial.

Follow Hill Street across the motorway and down to Molesworth Street. 'Lord Concrete', Francis Petre, completed the Basilica of the Sacred Heart in 1901. The Catholics took two years to build their church, but the Anglicans just along the road took over 40 to complete the bulky, blockish Wellington Cathedral of St Paul. The many fine windows include one by the Holm family, commemorating the merchant marine. For more information: www.cathedral.wellington.net.nz.

Forty-four years in the making, this imposing cathedral was designed by architect Cecil Wood to replace Old St Paul's (see page 21). He died in 1947, seven years before the Queen laid its foundation stone. In 1964 building was halted, incomplete, and was finished only as recently as 1998.

WELLINGTON 19

The Beehive (left), Parliament House (centre) and the Parliamentary Library (edge visible, right). This must be one of the few Parliaments in the world where you can picnic on the lawn.

'King Dick' Seddon, Lancashire-born, was a West Coast publican who had the sense to seem dumber than he was. From 1893 to 1906 he ruled 'God's Own Country' as he called it, like a one-man band.

Parliamentary Precinct Walk

Politics is Wellington's main employer and favourite blood sport. Parliament has sat here since 1865 but Parliament Grounds took on its modern look only in the 1920s, when work stopped on the central building in this complex, Parliament House. Parliament was actually called the General Assembly until 1951, when its upper house, or Legislative Council, was abolished. New Zealand is one of the few parliamentary democracies with neither state governments nor an upper house.

Head for the ground floor door of Parliament House, as it is the base for the free tours, which leave on the hour: Ph. 471-9503; www.ps.parliament.govt.nz/tour.htm. The Takaka marble building was built in a leisurely fashion between 1912 and 1922, to replace an older wooden structure burned down in 1908. If you think it looks lopsided, you are right. Architect John Campbell designed a matching wing south of the steps and a grand dome over the centre but, not for the first time, politicians trimmed costs. The elegantly spiky Gothic Revival Parliamentary Library (1899) next door lacks a storey, thanks to Premier Richard Seddon. Thomas Turnbull, the architect, was disgusted and asked to have his name removed from the foundation stone. Both old buildings were restored and strengthened in the 1990s (the tour will show you the state-of-the-art base isolation that protects against earthquakes).

Seddon stands in front, his arm stretched out, pontificating for

all he is worth. Just past his portly frame is the Executive Wing, or the Beehive, as everyone calls it, after its distinctive shape and a brand of matches. When Prime Minister Keith Holyoake sought advice in 1964, visiting British architect Sir Basil Spence quickly sketched out a rough design for this spectacular circular building, which local architects later struggled to make practical. It opened in 1981. Politicians hated it, but it has become a city icon.

Leave Parliament Grounds via the elegant 1913 northern gates. Cross Molesworth Street. This part of the Government Centre features several distinctive modern public buildings. There are two courts, the High Court back down the street past the pub and the Court of Appeal on this corner. Across the street, the National Library looks like a cross between a fortress and an upside-down wedding cake. Even if you are not interested in research, its exhibition gallery features interesting, free exhibitions on art, culture and history and is open weekdays, 9.00 am–5.00 pm, Saturday, 1.00 pm–4.30 pm, Sunday 1.00 pm–5.00 pm. More information: Ph. 474-3000; www.natlib.govt.nz.

Walk down Hill Street. Cross Mulgrave Street to Archives House. If it is open (weekdays, Saturday 9.00 am–1.00 pm), you can take in one of the changing historical exhibitions and visit The Constitution Room, where the rat-chewed, once-neglected Treaty of Waitangi now reposes in expensive splendour. Ph. 499-5595; www.archives.govt.nz.

Just north of Archives House another island of colonial Wellington cringes in the shadows of modern Wellington. Anglican House, as Bishopscourt (1879), was the old diocesan office and official residence for the Anglican bishop. Alongside is Old St Paul's. The Cathedral Church of St Paul, as it was first called, also served as the parish church

The National Library is one of the quality public buildings present in what is sometimes called the government centre. Its exhibition gallery is worth a look.

WELLINGTON

Left: To save costs Premier Richard Seddon cut a floor from the library building and John Campbell, the architect who replaced the indignant Thomas Turnbull, substituted gaol bricks (behind cement and plaster) to save money. It survived both the great fire of 1907 and one in 1992 while being restored. The statue in front is of another Liberal premier, John Ballance (1891–3), though whether it honours him is a moot point. It is such a bad likeness that a colleague complained 'such a statue adds a new terror to death'.

of Thorndon. Consecrated in 1866, it was designed in late Early English Gothic style by the Rev. Frederick Thatcher, noted for the churches he built for Bishop Selwyn. This, his finest work, was built in native timbers: totara, matai, rimu and kauri. It was altered and enlarged several times over the years by several architects including Christian Julius Toxward and Frederick de Jersey Clere. After the Second World War, the church built the big concrete St Paul's Cathedral on the corner of Hill and Molesworth Street and this building was saved only after a long and bitter campaign. Old St Paul's, as it became, is still used for weddings and funerals, but is managed by the Historic Places Trust and is open every day between 10.00 am and 5.00 pm. Step inside, as the interior is spectacular. Ph. 473-6722; www.historic.org.nz/index.html.

It has been said that wooden Victorian Gothic churches are New Zealand's greatest contribution to architecture. Old St Paul's has the finest interior, described by one architect as 'magnificent, like the upturned hull of a galleon'.
New Zealand Historic Places Trust

Retrace your steps and cross Mulgrave Street at the pedestrian crossing in front of Archives House. The Thistle Inn stands on the corner of Mulgrave Street and Kate Sheppard Place. One of 12 hotels opened in 1840, the Thistle is the oldest still trading from its original site, which was originally on the foreshore. Te Rauparaha was said to beach his canoe when he wet his whistle at the Thistle. The pub itself was burned and rebuilt in the 1860s, but is thought to include some original fabric. It was modernised in 2004.

Follow the path around the bus terminal and cross to the big wooden building on your left. Government Buildings has another link with Parliament, for here cabinet ministers once worked alongside their departmental officials. The Executive Council (the Governor-General and ministers) also met here in a special room now open to the public. When completed in 1876 on its own rectangular harbour reclamation, it housed the entire public service. It is the Victoria University law school now, but visitors are welcome and can see several rooms, including the Executive Council Room and a reconstructed vault (complete with rat!). The northern staircase is magnificent. The statue in the grounds is of wartime Prime Minister Peter Fraser rushing back to the House. Open Mon–Fri 9.00 am– 4.40 pm, Sat 10 am–3 pm.

Across the road at the edge of Lambton Quay is the Cenotaph (1931), the Wellington Citizens' War Memorial. 'Will to Peace', Richard Gross's mounted figure, rears up atop the column.

Government Buildings housed the entire public service in 1876. It is still the biggest wooden office building in the world, though not by choice, since the wood, made to look like stone, was an economy measure. Conserved by the Department of Conservation in the 1990s, the massive building features several historical displays.

Detail, Cenotaph.

Top: The tower blocks of Lambton Quay still follow the curve of 'the Beach', as the street was first known.

Above: Since 1976, 14 bronze plaques have marked the original shoreline from Thorndon to Oriental Bay.

A Walk along 'the Beach': Lambton Quay

Old Wellingtonians once talked about going down to 'the Beach' to shop. The reason becomes obvious when you notice the gentle curve of Lambton Quay. The cars and buses of the twenty-first century still follow the 1840s foreshore, then a spray-soaked beach where whisky-soaked traders peddled hooch from their tents. In 1845 Governor FitzRoy, never loved here, grumbled that the broken glass made it dangerous to walk along.

Cross to the seaward side of the Quay. The small park between Bowen and Ballance streets backs on to Pierre Finch Martineau Burrows's old (1880) Supreme Court building, whose main entrance is on Stout Street. The city's first large masonry public building signified that engineers felt they had mastered Wellington's shakes and quakes. Lately the High Court, in 2004 it began redevelopment as the new Supreme Court, replacing the Privy Council as the country's highest court.

A block along the Quay at its intersection with Stout Street is the old Public Trust Office, another earthquake pioneer, the first big

'Protoplasm', Phil Price's bright kinetic statue, bends in the breeze in front of the MLC building (1940), part of South Lambton Quay's reshaping as the financial heart of New Zealand between the wars. Just behind it, first the Old Bank Arcade and then the big black State Insurance Tower once housed the headquarters of the Bank of New Zealand.

public building with a 'skeleton riveted frame'. 'There is no stucco, no cheap make-believe about this office', Prime Minister Sir Joseph Ward announced when opening it in 1909. This swaggering, eccentric Elizabethan monument was saved in the 1980s after a long battle.

The building facing it was also 'saved', though the ghastly excrescence atop it may make you wonder why the Historic Places Trust bothered. The former State Insurance Building dates from 1940. Like its neighbour, the curvaceous Departmental Building, it epitomised the rapid growth of the state under Labour in the 1930s.

Just across Waring Taylor Street is a pocket park, once the site of the extraordinary Midland Hotel. Sheltered and sunny, handy to many eateries, Midland Park is a favourite with city workers.

Next is department store Kirkcaldie and Stains, a firm more dignified than its dead façade, three floors shoehorned where two once did business. But Kirk's, trading since 1863, is a Wellington institution, and recently bought the striking 1928 building in the next block, Harbour City Chambers.

Almost anything goes in Wellington City, where hideous additions blight many heritage buildings – even ones that, like the 1940 State Insurance Building, are supposedly protected by a Historic Places Trust heritage order.

The new tower tenanted by the Ministry of Foreign Affairs and Trade has facaded the old Hamilton Chambers and oozed into the 1926 T&G building. The ANZ's tiled and glass tower across Grey Street is also modern, but from this side of the street you will get good views of Cable Car Lane and the old Whitcombe and Tombs book and stationery store.

The final cluster in our walk recalls Wellington's phenomenal growth between the First and Second World Wars as the financial centre of New Zealand. The tiled tower on the corner was built as the MLC Centre in 1940, but is now mostly apartments, offices and shops. Opposite are a group of buildings also built for banks and insurance companies. The art deco Prudential Building was the most striking before developers 'improved it' in 2003–4.

Our final stop is the Old Bank Arcade. It consists of several buildings, built over a short period a hundred years ago and long the headquarters of the Bank of New Zealand. Left vacant after the bank occupied its 'Darth Vader's Pencil Box', the nearby black tower (now the State Insurance Tower), it was almost demolished before public money helped turn it into a mini Sydney-style Queen Victoria Building. Many of the elaborate banking chamber's details can be seen in the stylish centre's shops. But in keeping with Wellington's attitude to heritage, a 'highlight' of the centre is an historical clock, just inside the northern entrance. On the dot of the hour this kitsch, camp clock offers miniature moving tableaux of Wellington's history, including Katherine Mansfield making her arthritically jerky way along the Quay just past Daddy's bank.

For a reality check, head to the lower floor. In 1849 entrepreneur John Plimmer bought the wrecked *Inconstant* and beached her here as a warehouse. Roofed over, she was called 'Plimmer's Ark', serving until covered by later reclamations. Unearthed in the 1990s, part of the old hulk can be seen beneath plate glass, along with a mini museum. See: www.museumofwellington.co.nz/inconstant/index.html.

That ends our walk along 'the Beach', but if you are interested in Plimmer, Plimmer's Lane, opposite the arcade, has several Plimmer memorabilia. A bronze statue of the self-styled 'Father of Wellington' and dog Fritz stride towards the Quay and the lane features historic oaks and a memorial fountain.

Cuba Street and Courtenay Place Stroll

A hundred years ago Cuba Street was a major shopping street, as you will see if you look above the dreadful macrocarpa and steel verandahs to view the upper storeys of its classical two- and three-storey buildings. The street has its own heritage trail (look for the signs). In 1969, in the face of competition from the new suburban shopping centres, Lower Cuba Street became the country's first large pedestrian mall. Two subsequent makeovers have desexed that swinging 'sixties look, though the Bucket Fountain still delights children by noisily splashing the unwary, exactly as stuffy folk complained 30 years ago.

Left: Manners Mall, like lower Cuba Street, is a place to put on a show.

Right: The Bucket Fountain, the noisy, kitschy, splashy, beloved heart of Lower Cuba Street.

WELLINGTON

There are fewer 'suits' here than on Lambton Quay and more buskers. Cuba Street is as catholic as Auckland's K Road. Nationwide chain stores stake out the lower end, but things get more interesting the further up you go: fashion boutiques, restaurants, cafés, second-hand music, book and clothing shops, then finally adult stores and tattoo parlours.

Courtenay Place also used to be a major retail area. East of Te Aro Park (a controversially costly makeover most locals still call 'Pigeon Park'), restaurants, cafés, bars and theatres predominate. Virtually every cuisine and price bracket is catered for here, and in the side streets – Taranaki, Tory, Allen and Blair. The last two, until recently the home of warehouses and vegetable markets, are the city's prime grazing places.

And Courtenay Place is also the entertainment strip. Live performances can be enjoyed at the 1913 State Theatre, the Phoenix Theatre, the Westpac Saint James, Downstage and Bats. The city's cinema complexes include the Paramount, the historic Embassy Theatre and the new Reading complex.

Courtenay Place meets the slopes of Mount Victoria at Kent and Cambridge Terraces, turned into this wide thoroughfare after the 1855 earthquake quashed plans for a shipping canal. Bars blossom. The building in the traffic island was built as a public toilet in 1928, soon acquiring the nickname 'Taj Mahal'. On the southern side of the intersection, set back a respectful distance from the clubbers, Queen Victoria looks forever unamused.

Courtenay Place is dominated by the Embassy Theatre, restored in 2003 to host the world première of the Academy Award-winning Return of the King, *the third instalment of the* Lord of the Rings *trilogy. Courtenay Place is the city's theatre and café quarter. Behind it rises the dark green treetops of Mount Victoria.*

WELLINGTON

Wellington's views compensate for its steepness. A favourite vantage point is Mount Victoria, which can be reached by car via Alexandra Road, or by walking tracks from Oriental Parade and Majoribanks Street. 'Mount Vic' looks out over the eastern hills and harbour entrance (above) and the city (below). Set aside in 1841 for a 'public recreation ground for the inhabitants of Wellington' and part of the green Town Belt, Mount Victoria is popular with walkers, joggers and mountain bikers. A prominent memorial commemorates Antarctic explorer Admiral Richard Byrd.

WELLINGTON 31

3: Harbour City, Harbour Highlights

The harbour is one of Wellington's great attractions. In this chapter, we outline some ways that you can enjoy it, including walks, a boat trip and a drive.

Waterfront Walk

From the Railway Station, cross Waterloo Quay. Shed 21, converted to apartments, is the first of the big brick harbour board sheds we shall encounter. 'Shed' hardly does justice to these ornate buildings, for the harbour board, which ruled the roost here until 1989, did things in style. This is the southern end of the working port. Interisland ferries come and go, but the little wooden structure by the jetty used by the navy and the police once served the Eastbourne ferry.

Wellingtonians have fought for two decades over the waterfront, defeating the worst excesses of developers and their architect/urban designer lackeys. As you walk along the concrete Tug Wharf, 'Kumutoto' or the North Queens Wharf area, displays some of the most recent changes. 'Steamship Wharf', the strange-looking timber and iron building, is both old and new, as it is a twenty-first century import and heavy-handed remake of the historic Union Steam Ship Company building from Greta Point (see page 42). Behind it are two more harbour board sheds, William Fergusson's distinctive Sheds 11 and 13.

Queens Wharf has some claim to being the heart of the city. Over the last 140 years Wellington's first deep-water wharf has been altered, extended, redecked and partially infilled. It has seen Panama steamers, trans-Tasman liners, Nelson and Picton ferries and coasters of every type. It was once the city's front door. These days the cranes

Left: Taking in the late afternoon sun at Queens Wharf. The futuristic-looking crane is a Stothert & Pitt from the 1960s and is now a museum piece.

Although other users inhabit its office spaces, Wellington's railway station is the busiest in the country, serving both commuter and long distance passenger trains. Fletcher Construction built this colossus between 1933 and 1937. Architect Roger Walker thinks its style old-fashioned, but it was in keeping with that favoured for monumental public buildings of the day, such as the former Dominion Museum.

The brick harbour board 'sheds' have survived the changes on the waterfront and have been adapted to new uses. This is Shed 11, a twin of Shed 13, both completed in 1904 and given an Anglo-Dutch flourish above their doorways by William Fergusson. The Wharf Offices are in the background.

are museum pieces, the containers are signs and the only ships using it are high-profile sail training ships, cruise liners and sleek grey warships. But it is a great place to promenade, to catch the Days Bay/Somes Island ferry, to fish, kayak or simply just to people-watch from the restaurants and cafés.

The Harbourside Centre and the Events Centre are the twin blights that sparked a citizens' revolt against developers. The outer edge of the Events Centre, though, houses the first of the cultural sites on Queens Wharf Square, the Plimmer's Ark Museum, new home to the part of the wreck removed from under the Old Bank Arcade. See the wreck being conserved and read the displays on the history of the ship and the harbour. Open daily. Free admission. www.museumofwellington.co.nz/inconstant/index.html.

At the end of the Square, the Museum of Wellington City & Sea occupies the Bond Store. From the 1970s, a maritime museum spread throughout the building, which was strengthened and reopened in 1999. The museum's mission is now broader than maritime history. The ground floor houses a shop, a replica of part of the old bond store and changing exhibitions. The first floor tells the history of the harbour and the second floor examines the history of the city. Pride of place in the building is the old harbour board boardroom, preserved down to its tables and ornate chairs. Free admission. Ph. 472-8904; www.bondstore.co.nz.

The Wharf Offices (another Clere design) are now apartments, although the ground floor is a gallery for the New Zealand Academy of Fine Arts: Ph. 499-8807, free admission, open 10 am–5 pm during exhibitions; www.nzafa.com. Also, note the fine 1899 wrought-iron gates and the drinking fountain that honours 'Paddy the Wanderer', the dog who was such a part of the waterfront between 1928 and 1939 that the harbour board put him on its books as an assistant watchman. When he died, his admirers hired a taxi to take Paddy

WELLINGTON

The Museum of Wellington City & Sea, designed by Frederick de Jersey Clere in French Second Empire style, was built in 1892 to protect goods awaiting the payment of customs dues. The entrance display reconstructs that bond store look (look for the mechanical cat and rat).

Morning sun lights up the Wharf Offices, formerly 'Shed 7'. Frederick de Jersey Clere's waterfront masterpiece, they were designed in the elegant English classical style.

from the wharf to the crematorium!

Retrace your steps back to the water's edge and continue south. Frank Kitts Park, named after a timeserving mayor, was created in the 1970s during the last harbour board reclamations. The lagoon was enlarged again recently.

Instead of taking the striking new bridge across the lagoon, walk around the edge past Tanya Ashken's water sculpture and take the City to Sea bridge up to Civic Square, New Zealand's finest urban space. Civic Square is home to the city council, the Visitor Centre, the Michael Fowler Centre and the Town Hall, and three popular cultural institutions. The Wellington Public Library has plenty of

Waitangi Day celebration at Frank Kitts Park on the waterfront.

Several concrete writers' walk plaques cluster around the area of Frank Kitts Park and the museum. In this one sailor turned poet Denis Glover celebrates the tugs and the ships.

A tall mast from the Union Steam Ship Company's interisland ferry *Wahine*, which sank with the loss of 51 lives on 10 April 1968, towers above Frank Kitts Park.

WELLINGTON 37

Kayakers, rowers, dragon boaters and pedal boaters all use the lagoon. The Boatshed is a popular function venue.

Para Matchitt designed the carvings for the distinctive City to Sea bridge, which leads from the waterfront to Civic Square.

information about the city, internet terminals and a busy café. The City Gallery Wellington, in the old library building, hosts touring exhibitions; Ph. 801-3021 or website www.city-gallery.org.nz. Capital E, under the bridge, is a children's museum. Ph. 384-8502 or www.capitale.org.nz.

Take the funky City to Sea bridge back down past the southern edge of the lagoon. The bridge takes you past two historic wooden buildings, the 1885 Star Boating Club and Clere's 1894 Wellington Rowing Club. Both have been moved more than once (the Star Boating Club building was actually designed on iron tracks to make moving easier). The Rowing Club building's first occupants, the Wellington Naval Artillery Volunteers, used its odd little tower as an observation tower.

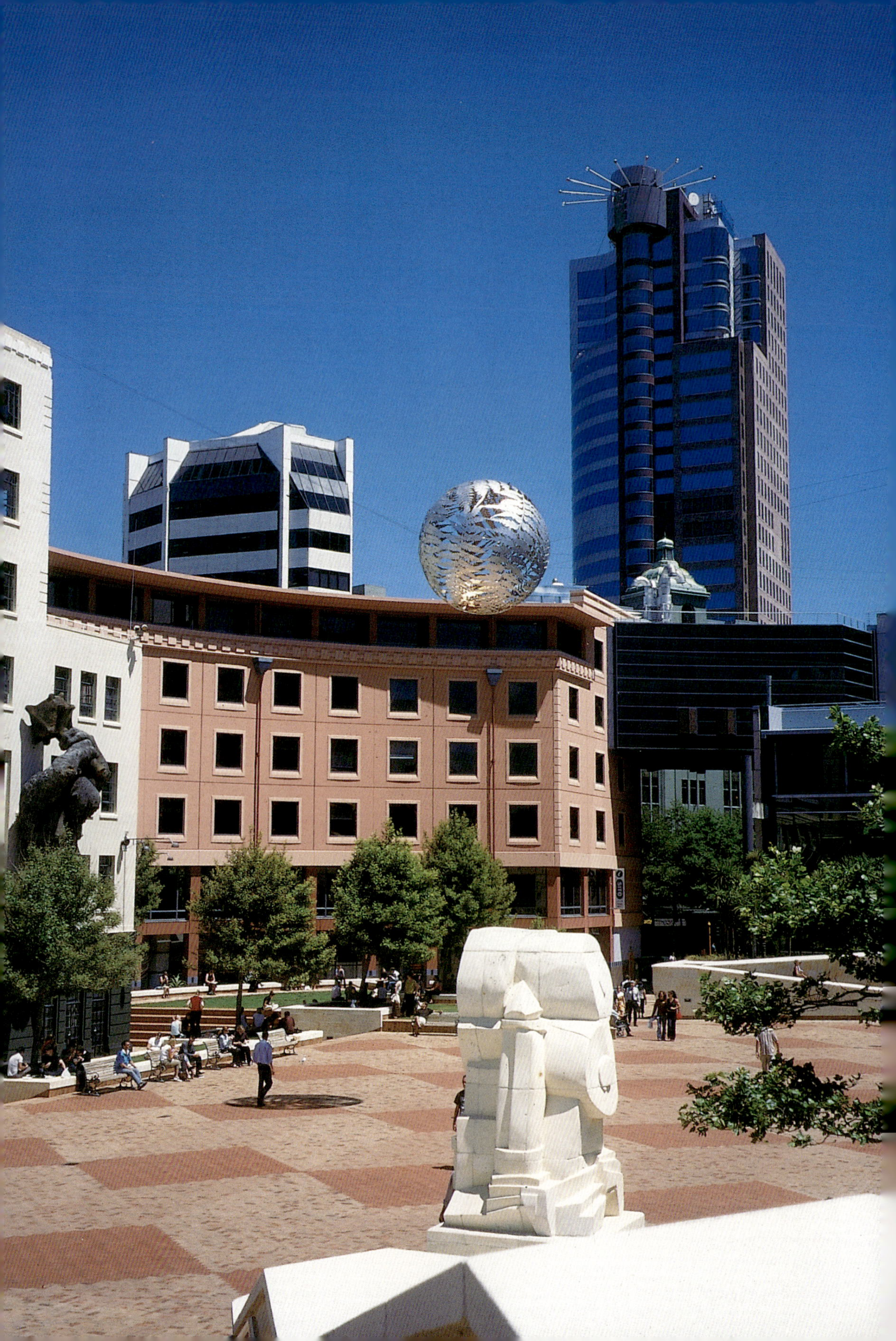

WELLINGTON

Located right on the waterfront, the Museum of New Zealand/Te Papa Tongarewa, is the country's most popular cultural institution.

Just behind on Taranaki Street Wharf is the Kupe Group statue (see page 6). The floating crane *Hikitia* dates from 1926 and still earns her keep with the odd heavy lift or salvage job. The area around Odlin Plaza (on your right) includes a number of new features such as the karaka grove, a boutique brewery in Shed 22 and the 1933 art deco Wellington Free Ambulance Building. Pity they butchered the tallest heritage building, Odlin's (1907), in its 2004 'redevelopment'.

Walk over the bascule bridge past the quirky little 1968 Tollhouse. Now run the gauntlet between the controversial 'Wharf Cutout' on your left (which offers expensive views of floating rubbish), and on your right Circa Theatre. Circa is the architectural equivalent of a high-speed train smash, the brutally mutilated, relocated façade of the old Westport Coal Company building butting up against a mediocrity that claims to pay homage to the Star Boating Club.

You are now at the entrance to the Museum of New Zealand/Te Papa Tongarewa. Te Papa, to use MONZ's brand name, opened here in 1998 after a fortune was spent on compacting the reclaimed land on the Union Company's old terminal. Down a small doorway to the

Left: Neill Dawson's shiny Sphere floats above Civic Square.

Right: South Korean drummers wow the crowd in the Te Papa courtyard. The museum stages many live cultural performances.

right of the main entrance a display explains base isolation earthquake technology.

Like most recent national museums, Te Papa was controversial. Architectural critics said it was as mediocre as a shopping mall, one practice offering to design a giant paua shell as an alternative! Others derided the interactive games, or thought that post-modern post-colonial pedants had taken over. Still more wondered where the old National Art Gallery collection had gone.

But the museum wowed the crowds from the first day and millions stream through its doors every year. It has done more than anything else to transform Wellington into a major tourist destination. Bush City in the front of the building takes visitors through caves, beaches and forests. The innards of the sprawling complex may be as mechanically stark as an aircraft carrier hangar deck, but they accommodate several floors of galleries – natural history, Maori, Pacific Islands, history and art, an eclectic mix of permanent and changing exhibitions. Popular highlights include the John Britten motorbike, a corrugated Holden station wagon, the 'Golden Days' nostalgia theatre set in a junkshop, an earthquake simulator, and racehorse Phar Lap's skeleton. Allow plenty of time. Admission is free (some touring exhibitions are charged for) and Te Papa is open every day of the year, 10 am to 6 pm (to 9 pm Thursdays). The fourth floor coffee shop is a great place to take a breather and the ground floor shop is one of the city's finest. Ph. 381-7000 or www.tepapa.govt.nz.

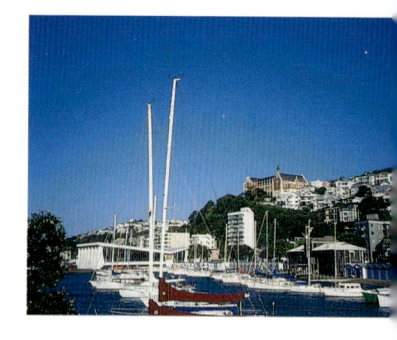

Mount Victoria from the Overseas Passenger Terminal, looking across the Clyde Quay boat harbour to the Freyberg Pool and St Gerard's monastery.

St Gerard's dominates the Mount Victoria skyline in this view from the top of the former band rotunda on Oriental Bay.

WELLINGTON

When you have had your fill, regain the 'harbour edge activity zone', as planner-speak has it, by the marina. The big art deco building on your right is Edmond Anscombe's 1939 Herd Street Post and Telegraph Building, now defiled and part of Waitangi Park (formerly Chaffers Park), the waterfront's newest development, begun in 2004 to incorporate a central field, wetlands, specialist gardens and buildings. The wharf is the Overseas Passenger Terminal, completed in 1973 just as the traditional liner trade to Europe died. On the other side is the historic Clyde Quay boat harbour, which dates from 1902. The little boatsheds date from 1905–6 and, in an age of gentler town planning, were made low so that they did not ruin the views of the neighbours. The Americans used them as a repair depot in the Second World War.

Continue past the Royal Port Nicholson Yacht Club along Oriental Parade. In early colonial times it was a rocky foreshore, used to cut up whales, but after the city completed the seawall in 1917, and began planting Norfolk pines, it became a desirable address and an inner city playground. Nature has had a fair help, the beach being built up artificially more than once. The Freyberg Pool (1963), named after a former governor-general, is one of the city's better twentieth-century structures. The beaches, redeveloped in 2003, are popular on hot days. A little further along the former band rotunda (1937), a restaurant since the 1980s, uses the 1917 platform as its base. The Norfolk pines are lit at night.

With its manicured golden sand, Oriental Bay hums on summer days. A restaurant operates from the old band rotunda.

Kayakers enjoy the sunshine off Point Jerningham. The container terminal and the stadium are in the distance.

Southern Coast Drive and Red Rocks Walk

Follow Oriental Bay Parade past the apartments, strollers, roller bladers and fishers out to Point Jerningham, named after Jerningham Wakefield, the adventurous, audacious, alcoholic son of Edward Gibbon Wakefield and author of the early classic *Adventure in New Zealand*. We are now in Evans Bay. Wind surfers love to barrel across the whitecaps in this natural wind tunnel. Several small beaches dot the western side, of which Balaena Bay is the most popular.

Little boxes made of ticky tacky now nuzzle up against the Crown marine research facilities at Greta Point, but at the southern end a jetty, giant cog and other traces of the old Wellington Patent Slip survive. From 1873 to 1985, large ships were hauled across the road to be repaired in the empty land under the cliffs.

At the marina at the end of Evans Bay Parade, turn left into Cobham Drive. The former governor-general it commemorates was renowned for his oratory, so it is fitting that the drive now celebrates windiness of another sort. Phil Price's 'Zephyrometer', a towering 26-metre orange tapered mast, swings about in the winds. At the other end of Cobham Drive in the roundabout by the airport turnoff, a second wind sculpture, Kon Dimopoulous's 'Pacific Grass', makes a striking sight when lit up at night.

Right: Zephyrometer, the 26-metre-long tapering orange wand, playfully salutes the city's 'Windy Wellington' reputation.

WELLINGTON 43

Balaena Bay is one of Evans Bay's small sheltered beaches.

Below: Large ships were once hauled across the road to the Evans Bay Patent Slip.

Turn left again. Most traffic takes the cutting into Miramar, but we shall follow the quieter Shelly Bay Road past the Miramar and Burnham wharves. This narrow, winding road passes through Shelly Bay, a former navy and later air force base. In the days when the big four-engine flying boats ruled the skies, Evans Bay was Wellington's international 'airport'.

Just past the base the road becomes Massey Road, a clue that we are approaching the tomb of William Massey, the gruff, bull-necked Ulster-born Auckland farmer who was Prime Minister from 1912 until his death in 1925. Left-wing historians have never much liked him, but the citizens of the day stumped up for this splendid Gummer and Ford and Samuel Hurst Seager-designed tomb atop Point Halswell, which Lord Bledisloe opened in 1930. It is worth parking carefully on the verge and taking the steepish track 200 metres up to the memorial for the views.

The Massey complex occupies the site of a Russian war scare coastal defence battery. The eastern side of the Miramar Peninsula was once thickly covered with coastal defence guns, searchlights and other shore defences. The ruins of Fort Ballance, named after another former prime minister, overlook Mahanga Bay.

There is nothing martial about this side of the peninsula now: Kau, Mahanga, Scorching, Karaka and Worser bays. Scorching Bay and Worser Bay are city favourites in summer. Why 'Worser'? It takes its name from an early harbour pilot, 'Worser' Hebberley, whose inevitable response to any question about the weather was that it would get 'worser'. Seatoun is a pleasant, pricey suburb, reputedly popular with the 'Wellywood' set during the filming of the *Lord of the Rings* series. The beaches are sheltered. At the southeastern end of Churchill Park off the Marine Parade in Seatoun, replica ventilators and an anchor and chain look out to Steeple Rock. The Wahine Memorial honours the people who died after the ferry *Wahine* foundered off the shore on 10 April 1968.

The shingly beach at Breaker Bay is popular with sunseekers.

Take Inglis Street through Seatoun, climb and crest the Pass of Branda and look out on the southern coast. The big bay on your right with the rock arch is Breaker Bay. It is shingle rather than sand, but is popular in summer, especially with people who like an all-over tan. The jagged points at the end are The Pinnacles. In line with them, just to the south of the bay, you will see Barrett Reef. It has claimed several ships, most recently the passenger ships *Wanganella* in 1947 and the *Wahine* in 1968. You will find another reminder just as you round the bend after the houses run out. At Palmer Head a small cairn and the bronze manoeuvring propeller from the ship commemorate the 51 people who lost their lives when the ship struck the reef, drifted off and foundered in a storm.

Tarakena Bay is popular with divers and boaties. Park in the Rangitatou Reserve car park on the right. You will see a red pou (carved post) which marks the site of the Ngai Tara pa wiped out in 1819–20, during the Musket Wars. Take the track up to another memorial, the Kemal Mustafa Ataturk Park and Memorial, honouring the founder of modern Turkey, who played a leading role in defeating Allied troops at Gallipoli in 1915. The ten-minute trek up to the memorial offers excellent views in several directions.

The Ataturk Memorial and park symbolise the friendship between former enemies. From here, you can see up the harbour past Barrett Reef and Breaker Bay in one direction, and out over Tarakena Bay and Cook Strait in the other.

WELLINGTON 45

The next highlight was high in more than one sense until recently. For almost a hundred years from 1898 the city's untreated sewerage was pumped out here at rocky, rugged, beautiful, Moa Point. The area is now being rehabilitated. The big cairn of turd-shaped rocks is called – what else? – 'Doo-Doos'.

Follow the Moa Point Road around the airport into the beautiful big halfmoon shape of Lyall Bay. Ever since the tram line reached there, Lyall Bay has been popular with Wellingtonians. Like most Cook Strait-facing beaches, the water temperature might most charitably be called 'bracing', but the beach is beautiful, sheltered from the northerlies and it has the added bonus of offering excellent plane and ship spotting. Surfers and board riders use it year-round.

From Lyall Bay you can watch the aircraft take off and land at the airport (rear, distance).

Below: Long before Wellington became such a multicultural place, Island Bay was made distinctive by the Italian and Greek fishing communities that earned their risky living off this wild coast.

Continue around the road through Houghton Bay to the seaside suburb of Island Bay. If you have a sense of déjà vu, that is probably because Rita Angus's painting of fishing boats bobbing in the chop has become an icon of New Zealand art. The island – Taputeranga – shelters boats and bathers alike. There is a playground just across the road. As you leave Island Bay, look out for two unusual houses on your right, one an old lighthouse, the other with a boat emerging from its upper storey!

Next up is Owhiro Bay, another attractive beach, with a public boat ramp that gets plenty of use from the divers who flock to this part of the coast.

Tinged their distinctive colour by iron oxide, the Red Rocks were formed about 200 million years ago by a submarine volcano.

The sealed road runs out by the car park near the old quarry site, now being transformed into Te Kopahau Reserve. This is the start of the popular Red Rocks Coastal Walk. Four-wheel drive vehicles can use the old shingle road, but it is popular with walkers, runners and cyclists. As you will have to ford the tiny Haape and Waipapa streamlets, wear practical footwear and carry appropriate clothing.

The walk goes for some distance around to Sinclair Head, but most people are satisfied with a shorter walk, an hour each way. We begin at the quarry site. The old benches on the hillsides can look magnificent when the afternoon sun highlights the marks the quarry workings have etched into them. About half way along the walk the rocks that give the place its name make themselves obvious. The walk takes you through two tiny clutches of classic baches. Just past the second group, about 2 km along, a signpost indicates a series of other walks.

Cross the Waipapa Stream and walk the short distance to the signposted seal colony. This spot is a winter 'haul-out' area for New Zealand fur seals during May to November when up to 80 males can be found here, resting from feeding as they build up condition for the breeding season. The distinctive cutting just above the haul-out area is the Devil's Gate. Sinclair Head is about another hour's walk, but many people end their walk here. You are about an hour away from the car park.

Return to the city via either Happy Valley Road and Brooklyn, or The Parade through Island Bay and Adelaide Road through Newtown.

The Devil's Gate is just past the seal haul-out. When walking up it, watch out for four-wheel drive vehicles coming the other way.

Owhiro Bay car park.

A handful of traditional baches survives.

WELLINGTON 47

A yacht lies off the Matiu/Somes Island lighthouse. The trip takes 10–15 minutes, the only traffic delays being pleasant ones, caused by the dolphins that like to play off the ferry's bow.

Boat Trip to Matiu/Somes Island

Just 8 km from the city centre, Somes Island is an ancient place of defence and of detention. The defence has been against invaders, disease in the case of immigrants (1870s to 1920s), then animals, which were quarantined here until the mid 1990s. Other detainees have included 'enemy aliens': New Zealanders of German or Italian extraction during the world wars. David McGill named his history of Somes *Islands of Secrets* and Maurice Gee set his novel *Live Bodies* here.

These days the live bodies are insects, birds and lizards, all cared for by DOC, which has rid the island of predators. It is New Zealand's most accessible island sanctuary, a rare toehold for tuatara. DOC has also re-established Cook Strait giant weta and kakariki (red-crowned parakeet). The island has one of only two breeding colonies of spotted shag in the Wellington region.

Take the harbour ferry from Queens Wharf. Prior booking is advisable (but not essential), especially in summer when seats fill up quickly or when the island is sometimes closed because of fire danger.

The DOC information centre has sheets on aspects of the island's history and wildlife, and maps. Only one quarantine building remains, but there are plenty of reminders of the island's past: a memorial just past the wharf, the emplacements for the four 3.7-inch anti-aircraft guns installed there during the Second World War and the lighthouse, built in 1900 to replace an 1866 structure. The island was named after Joseph Somes, deputy governor of the New Zealand Company, and was officially renamed Matiu/Somes Island in 1997.

The ferry landing at Matiu/Somes Island. Ferries come and go every two hours, giving you plenty of time to do the Circuit Track (just over an hour). Take food and drink if you want to make a day of it. There is no swimming beach and no pets are allowed.

Eastern Bays Excursion

This outing consists of a leisurely drive to Eastbourne, where you might have lunch or a cup of tea or coffee, and a walk along the coast towards the Pencarrow Lighthouse if the weather is favourable.

Waterloo Quay takes us past the railway station through the port area, with its container stacks and log piles. That big round thing on your left is not an overgrown oil tank, it is the Westpac Wellington Stadium, more commonly called 'the Cake Tin'. When the 'full house' sign is put out, there are 34,500 bums on seats here for rugby, cricket or rock concerts.

Aotea Quay whizzes us past the log ships, laid-up trawlers and interisland ferries out on to the Hutt Road. People have spent millions on building up the road, motorway and rail links, but this vital link to the Hutt Valley got its biggest hand-up from the 1855 earthquake, which widened a narrow and unsatisfactory harbour fringe.

At Petone turn on to The Esplanade. Until 30 years ago Petone was synonymous with pollution from the freezing works and the other factories that pumped as much muck as brass into the community. Most have now gone and the beach is better for that, offering cleaner water and attractive harbour views. Just past the long wharf, once used by small coasters, the Petone Settlers' Museum occupies the striking white art deco building by the foreshore. Opened with great fanfare in 1940, this was the Wellington Provincial Centennial Memorial. Open 12 noon–4 pm Tuesday to Friday, weekends and

A 'Welling Tin', 'the Cake Tin'… whatever you call it, Wellingtonians have warmed to the Westpac Stadium. Oriental Bay and Mount Victoria are in the background.

Right: Buick Street, looking back over Louise Purvis's 7-metre tall Te Puna Wai Ora (The Spring of Life) to the Settlers' Museum and the harbour. You can draw artesian water from the sculpture, which celebrates the Hutt aquifer that sustains life in the capital. Petone street names honour early migrant ships and settlers.

The bow of the immigrant ship Aurora projects from the front of the Settlers' Museum. It is a triumphant salute to colonisation, the building whitewashed European settlement in the romanticised figures of a Maori chief welcoming an immigrant family etched into the big display window. Inside an innovative little museum tells more nuanced local and migration history with panache.

public holidays 1 pm–5 pm. Entry by donation. Ph. 568-8373 or www.huttcity.govt.nz. Just past the Museum is a cross, another centennial memorial, in this case the Presbyterian Church's, and a bit further along two giant oars, 'Salute', a piece by John Calvert on the site of the first settlers' landing.

Turn into Buick Street (named after an early settler, not the car) and head up to Jackson Street. A few years ago Jackson Street, Petone's main shopping street, took a bit of a battering from the big malls and discount stores that opened in nearby Lower Hutt, but the locals fought back and breathed new life into their precinct. With its small-scale heritage buildings, many of which now house specialty shops and agreeable cafés, the restored gaol and police station and the sporting champions plaques in the footpath, Petone is worth the journey.

The harbour ferry still uses the Day's Bay wharf. The bay, redolent with Katherine Mansfield associations, has a sheltered beach, cafés and galleries and is a popular excursion destination. Eastbourne village can be seen in the distance.

To return to The Esplanade, turn right into Patrick Street which features several well-maintained houses built by the Liberal government about 100 years ago, known as 'Seddon's State Houses'.

Follow The Esplanade into Waione Street and cross the bridge over the Hutt River and follow Seaview Road through the industrial area. We pass the tanker terminal at Point Howard and then follow Marine Drive through the more graceful eastern bays – Lowry, York, Mahina, Days and Rona Bays. They are largely residential, sheltered, leafy and desirable retreats for city workers.

Days Bay has been a popular excursion destination for well over a century. The harbour ferry still calls at the Days Bay Wharf and city

The bush-clad eastern bays are highly desired residential areas.

WELLINGTON 51

The 1858 lighthouse at Pencarrow Head was New Zealand's first permanent tower and the only one ever kept by a woman, Mary Jane Bennett. Spare a thought for her and her late husband. 'The house is neither wind nor waterproof', he complained. 'The stove is of very little use. I have been four days without being able to boil the kettle inside or out'. In really strong winds, the Bennetts took refuge in a nearby cave.
New Zealand Historic Places Trust

The Pencarrow walkway offers many interesting attractions. Since it can be 'bracing' in either a southerly or a northerly, take water and a change of clothes.

dwellers still picnic at Williams Park, just as they did in the days of steam ferries, brass bands and scratchy woollen bathing costumes. The Pavilion is not the original, but it continues an old tradition. Behind the park a loop track offers a two-hour trek up through the forest, native trees up the top and a Depression-era pine forest back on the other side.

Eastbourne is a pleasant, leafy township, full of galleries and cafés. Follow the road to where it ends just past the art deco omnibus depot. A signpost near Burdans Gate No. 1 lists the attractions of the route – the shipwreck sites, wharf remains and lighthouses, amongst other things – and the time that it will take to get to them. On a fine day it is a great walk, enlivened by ships passing in and out of the harbour, but carry warm clothing; the weather can be changeable on this beautiful, bleak coast.

THIS MONUMENT IS DEDI-
CATED TO THE MEMORY OF
HENRY EDMUND HOLLAND
LEADER OF THE LABOUR PARTY
1919-33. TO COMMEMORATE
HIS WORK FOR HUMANITY.
HE DEVOTED HIS LIFE TO
FREE THE WORLD FROM
UNHAPPINESS, TYRANNY AND
OPPRESSION

4: The Best of the Rest

MUSEUMS, GALLERIES AND HISTORIC PLACES

Want to see more places? Here are some more leading attractions within easy walking distance of our walks and drives.

Bolton Street Memorial Park
Bolton Street, just off The Terrace

You can enter this park from Anderson Park at the north-eastern end of the Botanic Garden or from Bolton Street, just off The Terrace. The Bolton Street Memorial Park is what survived after the urban motorway was thrust through the historic cemetery (the Catholic section is marooned up in Mount Street, by the university) 40 years ago, against vigorous protests. It is now popular with office workers, who enjoy its open spaces and the hundreds of heritage roses. Displays in the replica of the 1866 Anglican mortuary chapel list the 3700 people disinterred and explain the history of the cemetery. With the aid of pamphlets you can find the graves of some of colonial New Zealand's leading lights, including the Wakefields.

Wellington being Wellington, politicians loom large even in death. For two of the bigger noises, take the footbridge across the motorway and follow Robertson Way up to the soaring Seddon Memorial, another tribute to King Dick. But what would gruff socialist firebrand Labour Party leader Harry Holland have thought of Richard Gross's homoerotic memorial to him?

Opposite: When the prim and proper criticised the appropriateness of nudity in a memorial to a politician, sculptor Richard Gross replied that his statue symbolised the efforts of Man, and Harry Holland in particular, to rise above the primeval slime and reach heights of spiritual achievement.

Below: The Sexton's Cottage dates from 1857 and is one of the city's oldest surviving buildings.

Katherine Mansfield Birthplace

25 Tinakori Road, Thorndon

Banker Sir Harold Beauchamp and his family lived in this 1880 house from 1888 to 1893. Another celebrity occupant, Plunket Society founder Dr Truby King, lived here between 1921 and 1924. Now managed by the Katherine Mansfield Birthplace Society, which has restored the house and garden, this award-winning house museum tells the story of New Zealand's most famous author. Open every day except for Mondays, Good Friday and Christmas Day. Admission charges. Ph. 473-7268.

Colonial Cottage Museum

68 Nairn Street, Te Aro (near the top of Willis Street)

Carpenter and timber merchant William Wallis built this steep-roofed colonial Georgian cottage in 1858 shortly after he and new bride Catherine landed at Wellington. They had ten children, seven of whom lived here. The cottage remained in family ownership for 119 years. It survives thanks to granddaughter Winifred Turner, who fought plans for its demolition when in her 70s. Eventually the council helped the Colonial Cottage Museum Society and the Historic Places Trust to restore the house. Admission charges apply. Open 12 noon–4 pm Boxing Day to 30 April, 12 noon–4 pm winter. Ph. 384-9122 or www.colonialcottagemuseum.co.nz.

Wellington has never forgotten Katherine Mansfield. Her birthplace in Thorndon is a popular visitor attraction.

More Walks

The Wellington City Council has designated four major walkways for strollers, three of which take four to five hours. These include the Southern Walkway, from Oriental Bay over Mount Victoria to Island Bay. Information about the walks can be found in an Explore Wellington brochure from the Visitor Centre in Civic Square, or at www.wellingtonnz.com/SightsAndActivities/Walks.

Fully furnished, the Colonial Cottage in Nairn Street reflects the 1870s, when its owners had the money to add a front verandah, rear kitchen, toilet and wash house to the original plain four-roomed box.

Adam Art Gallery, Victoria University

The Adam Art Gallery is a striking modern structure nestled between the Old Kirk Building and the Student Union, via Gate 3 of the Kelburn Parade entrance to the university's main campus. It is within easy (albeit steepish in places) walking distance of the city and can be reached by bus (Numbers 17, 18, 20, 22 and 23) or from the University stop on the Cable Car, followed by a short walk along Salamanca Road. Ph. 463-5489 or 463-5229, or www.vuw.ac.nz/adamartgal.

Open 11 am to 5 pm on Tuesdays to Sundays except public holidays, the Adam Art Gallery is housed in a modern Athfield-designed building. Entry is by donation. Also of interest are the university's art collection, displayed in the foyers of many of the buildings, as well as the restored Hunter Building to the north of the gallery and the Mount Street Cemetery on the seaward side of the pathway.

National War Memorial, Carillon and Tomb of the Unknown Warrior

Buckle Street, City

In 1919 the government decided to build a national war memorial but, for various reasons, it was 1928 before it authorised turning this Mount Cook site into an art gallery, museum, and 49-bell carillon. The Massey University now uses the grey, sombre bulk of the former Dominion Museum, but the rest of the site remains the nation's primary memorial to the dead of our foreign wars.

Architects Gummer and Ford built the museum in a heavy, stripped classical style, but let their hair down with the 50-metre tall carillon, which is a rakishly art deco 'erect phallic shape'. Thousands of Wellingtonians turned up for its dedication on Anzac Day 1932, when Governor-General Lord Bledisloe switched on the Lamp of Remembrance atop the tower and the *Evening Post* reported hearing 'magic from the skies'.

What is a carillon (pronounced 'ká-ri-lon')? Basically, it is a huge set of cast bronze bells. They are hung stationary in a massive steel framework and are struck by cast-iron clappers, which are operated by wires attached to a manually played keyboard. The carillonist quite literally goes like the clappers, striking the wooden keys of the keyboard with clenched fists and by depressing the foot pedals. The sound varies according to how hard each bell is struck. Since 1984, the carillon has been substantially rebuilt and enlarged and its total range has been extended to six octaves. With its 74 bells, Wellington's carillon is the third largest in the world by total weight.

The Hall of Memories took longer to build. Plans were prepared in 1937, and Gummer and Ford forwarded a new set in 1949, but the project was not finished until 1964. Step inside this peaceful place, where quiet recesses commemorate the services and campaigns. Four Rolls of Honour list the 28,654 New Zealanders who have died in conflicts from the Boer War to the Vietnam War. Lyndon Smith's bronze statue of a family group sets the tone.

In 2004, after some controversy, the Ministry for Culture and Heritage added a Tomb of the Unknown Warrior to the forecourt. In Kingsley Baird's restrained 'Beneath the Southern Cross', the light grey Takaka marble crosses represent the warrior's companions who remain buried overseas; the distance of the foreign land he left behind is represented on the base of the tomb by a night sky of black granite.

The National War Memorial is open daily except on Christmas Day and Good Friday. Mon–Sat: 10.30 am–4.30 pm; Sun: 12.30 pm–4.30 pm. Free admission. Website: www.nationalwarmemorial.govt.nz/index.html.

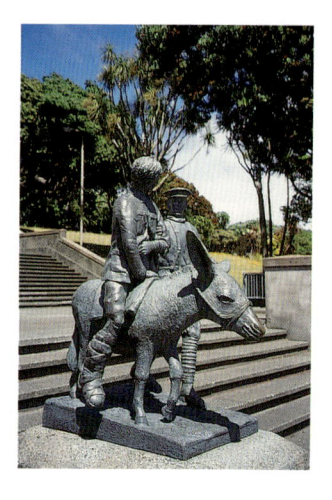

The RSA commissioned this bronze statue of Henderson and his donkey to commemorate the heroic stretcher-bearers of the Gallipoli campaign.

Opposite: Gummer and Ford's 50-metre carillon tower.

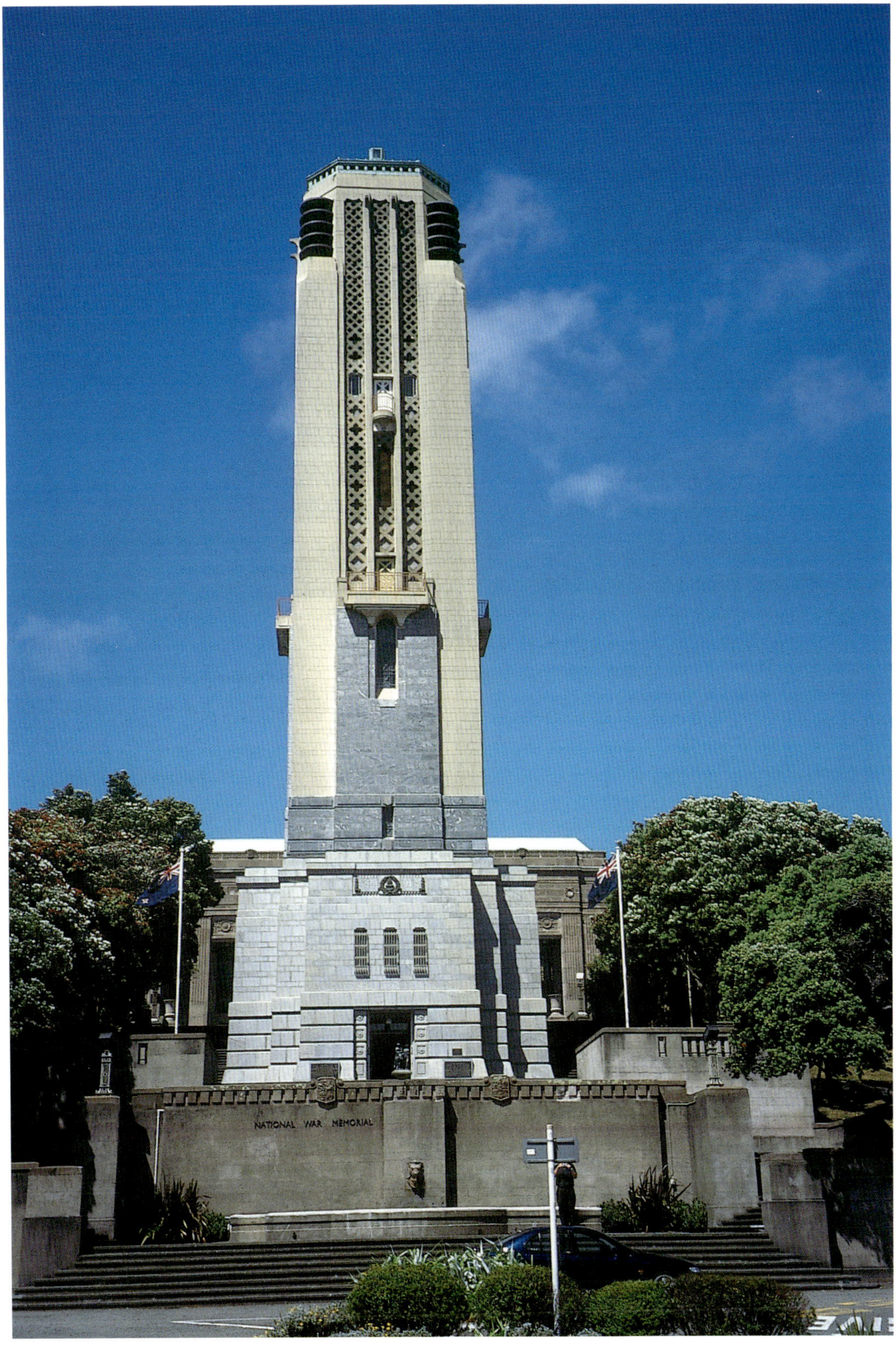
NATIONAL WAR MEMORIAL

Basin Reserve and National Cricket Museum

The Old Grandstand, Basin Reserve

The Basin Reserve got its name because an early plan had a shipping channel leading up swampy Kent/Cambridge Terrace to an enclosed shipping basin here. Why anyone would bother when Lambton Harbour offered sheltered deep water is a mystery, but the 1855 earthquake sank those plans by raising the land another couple of metres.

Several sports have used the Basin but it is internationally famous as a test cricket venue. Since 1987 the Old Stand (1924) has been a superb repository of cricketing life, lore and some legend. Admission to the Basin Reserve is free when games are not in progress. Admission charges apply to the Museum, which is open 10.30 am–3.30 pm over summer (and all day during games). Ph. 385-6602.

The Museum Stand (centre) at Basin Reserve houses the National Cricket Museum. In the background are (left) the Wellington campus of Massey University (formerly the Dominion Museum) and the National Carillon.

The Victorian-era Karori Reservoir valve tower. The urban sanctuary occupies a valley that supplied water to the city until the 1990s. The bush has been regenerating since the early 1900s. Displays in the neighbouring boatshed tell the history of the reservoir.

NATURE AND NURTURE

In addition to its natural wild places, in the hills and on the coast, Wellington is rich in wildlife sanctuaries close to the city centre.

Karori Wildlife Sanctuary

Waiapu Road, Karori

Driving from the city, take Glenmore Street, turn left at the Kelburn viaduct roundabout and continue through the Karori Tunnel. Waiapu Road is the first on the left after leaving the tunnel. Or take the bus to Appleton park, alight at the first stop after the tunnel, then take a brief walk to the Sanctuary. Bus Nos 12, 17 (peak hours), 18, 22 or 23.

The Karori Wildlife Sanctuary is a decade into what will be its 500-year journey, by the time many of its trees have matured. Although this is the world's first urban wildlife sanctuary, it does not overlook historic heritage, as you discover when you enter the gates. Features include the valve tower and boatshed from the old reservoir, a dam and the Morning Star and Union goldmines.

The statistics are impressive: 35 km of bush tracks and 252 ha of forest, streams and lakes, all behind an 8.6-km long, $2.2 million fence that not even a mouse can get through. Tracks are graded into road/path (the easiest), walking and tramping (the steepest). All tracks are well signposted, rest areas abound and there is plenty of information on the birds, trees and fish. Birds you may see or hear include weka, kaka, miromiro, fantails, tui, brown teal, North Island saddleback, bellbirds and whiteheads. Nocturnal little spotted kiwi are also here, along with weta.

Allow at least two hours for the tamest circuit around the lakes, much longer if you want to tackle the steeper tracks, one of which skirts the Brooklyn wind turbine.

Open every day of the year except Christmas Day. Admission charges apply. You can also pre-book for special nocturnal guided tours when Nature is at its throatiest. Ph. 920-9200 or www.sanctuary.org.nz.

Otari–Wilton's Bush

Wilton Road, between Gloucester and Warwick Streets. The No. 14 bus stops at the reserve.

Walk 18 m above the forest floor on a canopy walkway while native birds fly overhead at the only large botanic garden in New Zealand dedicated solely to native plants. There are 100 ha of native plants and a further five of plant collections at Otari–Wilton's Bush on the western slopes of the city. Otari ('place of snares') was used by Maori for hunting and we are fortunate that early settler Job Wilton fenced off part of the forest, which became known as Wilton's Bush.

In 1926 the Otari Open Air Plant Museum was established by J.G. McKenzie and the country's leading biologist, Leonard Cockayne. Thanks to them, you can now see over 1200 plant species, ranging from sub-Antarctic hardies to natives of the islands to the north of New Zealand. It is still a research station.

Otari–Wilton's Bush is open between sunrise and sunset (information centre 9 am to 5 pm), is well signposted and includes a picnic area. Free admission.

Some of the luxuriant plant life in the unique Otari-Wilton's Bush plant museum.

WELLINGTON

Visitors stream into the Wellington Zoo entrance and shop.

Wellington Zoo
200 Daniell Street, Newtown

The inner-city suburb of Newtown is a vibrant multicultural community and the base for the city's main hospital complex. If driving, take Kent Terrace, go round the Basin Reserve, follow Adelaide Road and Riddiford Street past the shopping centre and turn left into Roy Street. Alternatively, take a No. 10 or 23 bus.

In 1906 a circus presented a young lion to the city. 'King Dick' (named after the late premier) lived at the Botanic Garden until the council started developing part of Newtown Park as New Zealand's first zoo in 1907. The Zoo no longer keeps elephants in its historic Elephant House but it has many of the other exotic crowd-pleasers – giraffes, lions, Sumatran tigers, Malayan sun bears, chimpanzees, baboons, and show-stealing otters and meerkats. In keeping with modern practice, Wellington Zoo emphasises conservation, breeding some exotic mammals as well as native birds such as brown teal, Campbell Island teal and parakeets for DOC and for the Karori Sanctuary. The new nocturnal enclosure, 'Te Ao Mahina – The Twilight', features kiwi, morepork and tuatara.

Guides are helpful and knowledgeable. There is a shop, food kiosk and toilet facilities. Open every day except Christmas Day. Admission charges apply. Open 9.30 am–5 pm every day except Christmas Day. Ph. 381–6755 or www.wellingtonzoo.com.

WELLINGTON 63

Wellington Botanic Gardens

KEY
- Visitor Centre
- Public Toilet
- Lookout
- Main Paths
- Native Bush

Opposite: At the zoo feeding time for the giraffes is always popular.

Above: Map of the Botanic Garden.

Below: The dragon boat festival every March is just one of many events on Wellington's crowded calendar of cultural events.

FURTHER AFIELD

Several fine museums and galleries can be found further away from the Wellington City/Petone areas.

Dowse Art Museum

Laings Road, Lower Hutt, Ph. 570-6500; www.huttcity.govt.nz/services/dowse.shtml. Open Mon to Fri 10 am–4 pm; Sat, Sun and public holidays 11 am–5 pm. Free except touring exhibitions. Take a No. 83 bus from Wellington. The Dowse exhibits New Zealand art, craft and design in innovative ways.

Pataka Porirua Museum of Arts and Cultures

Cnr Norrie and Parumoana streets, Porirua. Ph. 237-1511. Open Mon to Sat 10 am–4.30 pm, Sun 11 am–4.30 pm. Free except for Melody Farm, a musical gallery.

In addition to exhibiting local Porirua history, Pataka showcases modern Maori, Pacific Islands and New Zealand European artists.

Southward Car Museum

Otaihanga Road, 3 km north of Paraparaumu. Ph. 297-1221 or www.southward.org.nz/. Open 9.00 am–4.30 pm every day except Good Friday, Anzac Day morning and Christmas Day.

Founded by Sir Len Southward, the Southward Car Museum is crammed with cars, motorbikes, bicycles, fire engines and aircraft. Everything from a Model T to a De Lorean, with a Nazi Mercedes Benz and a gangster car in between!

Half the city's population seems to cram into Tinakori Road every year for the annual Thorndon Fair.

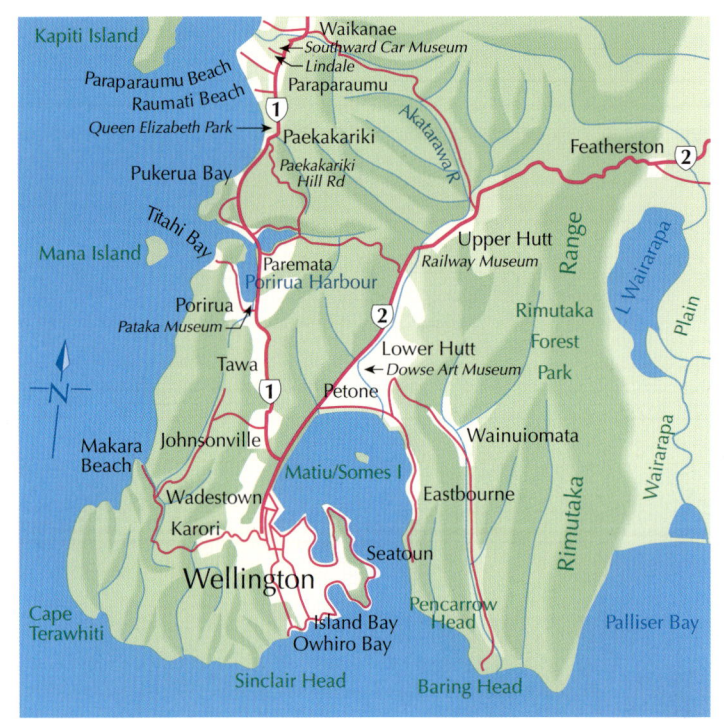

Wellington region.